Contemporary Bible Series
JESUS Does Miracles and Heals People
Retold by Joy Melissa Jensen
Published by
Scandinavia Publishing House 2010
Drejervej 15,3   DK-2400 Copenhagen NV
Denmark
E-mail: info@sph.a
Web: www.sph.a

Text copyrigh
© Scandinavia Publishing Hous
Illustrations copyright © Gustavo Maza
Design by Ben Ale
Printed in Chin
ISBN 978 87 7247 693

JESUS
Does Miracles and Heals People
Retold for Children

by Joy Melissa Jensen

scandinavia

Contents

A Man with a Crippled Hand

Mark 3:1-6

On Sunday Jesus went into the temple to worship. The Pharisees whispered to each other, "Let's see if we can catch Jesus doing something wrong." They watched him very closely. If only they could catch Jesus healing somebody, they could accuse him of working on a Sunday. But Jesus knew what the Pharisees were thinking. So he invited a man with a crippled hand to stand up. Then Jesus faced the crowd and said, "On a Sunday should we do good deeds or bad deeds? If we can save a life, shouldn't we do it?" But none of the people said a word. Jesus was disappointed. He felt sorry for them because they still did not understand. "Stretch out your hand," he said to the man. The man obeyed and his crippled hand was healed. "Jesus is a criminal," the Pharisees said to each other. "He healed someone on the Sabbath!" So they began to plot against him.

5

A Sick Woman

Mark 5:21-34

Jesus went to teach by the shore of Lake Galilee. A man named Jairus had come to see Jesus. He had a sick daughter. He told Jesus, "Please come back to my home! My daughter may die any minute." So Jesus went with him, and all Jesus' followers came too. While they were walking, a woman tried to get Jesus' attention. But there were so many people around him that it was hopeless. She was very sick. She had spent all her life going to doctors. Not one of them could heal her sickness. "If I can just touch his clothes," she said to herself, "I will get well." So she brushed her hand along his robe. In an instant, all her sickness left her, and she was well.

Jesus felt power go out from him. "Who touched my clothes?" he asked. His disciples told him, "Jesus, there are so many people here. How can you ask who touched you?" But the woman knew that Jesus was talking about her. She started to tremble as she knelt down before him. She told him about her sickness and why she had touched his clothes. So Jesus said to her, "You had faith, and your faith is what healed you!"

The woman smiled. She was not afraid anymore.

6

A Dying Girl

Mark 5:35-43

Finally Jesus reached Jairus' home. Some men came out of the house and told Jairus, "It's too late. Your daughter is dead." But Jesus didn't listen to them. He told Jairus, "Don't worry. Just have faith!" Then he went inside the house. The little girl's family were sitting around crying. "Why are you so sad?" Jesus asked them. "The girl is only asleep."

Jesus went into the girl's bedroom. He picked up her hand and said, "Talitha, koum!" which means, "Little girl, get up!" Suddenly the little girl opened her eyes and sat up. She got out of bed and started walking around. Her parents were amazed. Jesus told them to give the little girl something to eat. "But keep this miracle that you have seen to yourself," Jesus added. "Don't tell anyone." Then he left.

The Storm

Mark 4:35-38

Jesus was with his disciples on Lake Galilee. The sky was growing dark, and Jesus said, "Let's cross to the east side." While they were crossing, a windstorm started to blow. Waves splashed and filled the inside of the boat with water. The boat got heavier and heavier and started to sink. "Jesus, help us!" the disciples cried. But Jesus was asleep at the back of the boat. He didn't hear them. The storm was growing worse. So they shook Jesus and woke him up, "Teacher," they said, "don't you care that we are about to drown?"

Jesus Calms the Storm

Mark 4:39-41

When Jesus woke up, he didn't panic like the disciples. He stood up and held out his hand. Then he told the waves, "Be quiet!" And he told the wind, "Be still!" All at once the sea stopped thrashing and the wind stopped howling. It was calm and peaceful again.

Jesus turned back around to his disciples and said, "Why were you afraid? Don't you have faith?" But the disciples became even more afraid. "Who are you?" they asked. "Who is this? Even the wind and the waves obey him!"

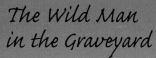

The Wild Man in the Graveyard

Mark 5:1-20

Jesus and his disciples crossed Lake Galilee in their boat. They started to get out when they spotted a man running towards them. He had been living in the graveyard. He was dirty and covered in cuts and bruises. People from the town had tried to lock him away. They put chains around his legs and arms, but he always

14

broke them.

When the wild man saw Jesus, he came and knelt down before him. "What's your name?" Jesus asked him. "My name is Lots— because I've got lots of evil spirits inside of me." Jesus wanted to help the man. But the man said, "Don't get rid of my evil spirits, just send them into those pigs!" He pointed at a herd of pigs up on the hill. So Jesus sent the man's evil spirits into the pigs. The whole herd went wild and rushed down the hill straight into the lake. All the pigs drowned. The pig farmers couldn't believe it. They went into town to tell the people. But the man bowed before Jesus. "Please let me come with you," he said. Jesus told him, "Go home to your family. Tell them how much the Lord has done for you."

The man spent the rest of his life teaching people about Jesus.

Jesus Heals Two Blind Men

Matthew 9:27-31

Jesus was walking along when two blind men started to follow him. They were shouting, "Have pity on us, Son of David!" Jesus started to go indoors but the blind men did not go away. So Jesus turned around and asked them, "Do you believe I can make you well?"

"Yes, Lord," they answered.

So Jesus laid his hands on their eyes. He said, "Because of your faith, you are healed." Then he took his hands away. The men looked around and saw everything. "Praise God, we're healed!" they shouted with joy. Jesus told them, "Don't tell anyone about what I have done." But the men were too excited to listen. They ran off and told everybody they could find about how Jesus healed them.

Herodias Takes Revenge

Mark 6:14-29

King Herod married a woman named Herodias. But she was his brother's wife. John the Baptist told the king, "It isn't right for you to marry your brother's wife." Herodias didn't like John. "Who are you to judge the king and queen?" she said to him. Then she asked Herod to kill him. But Herod knew that John was a holy man. He didn't want to kill him, so he just threw him in jail.

On Herod's birthday he threw a big party. The daughter of Herodias came in and danced for the guests. They all smiled and clapped after she was done. "Dear girl," said Herod, "You've made us so happy. Ask for anything you want, and I will give it to you." The girl didn't know what to say, so she ran back to her mother. Herodias told her, "Ask the king for the head of John the Baptist."

So the girl went back and told Herod what she wanted. The king bowed his head. He was sorry for what he had said. But he kept his promise. "Cut off John's head," he told his jail guards. And when this was done, the girl took the head of John the Baptist to her mother. Herodias was very pleased. But John's followers were sad, and Jesus was too. They took his body and put it into a tomb.

The Work of Jesus' Followers

Luke 10:1-12

The Lord picked seventy-two followers to go out and spread his message. He sent them two by two to every town and village. He told them, "Don't take anything with you, not even sandals. If someone invites you into their home, say, 'God bless this home with peace.' If they are kind to you, your prayer of peace will bless them. Eat whatever they give you and heal anyone

who is sick. Tell them, 'God's kingdom is coming soon!'"

Jesus' followers obeyed. When they came back, they were very excited and ran to Jesus. "Lord," they told him, "even the evil spirits listened to us when we spoke your name!" Jesus smiled. "Are you so surprised?" he asked. "If you believe in me, nothing can harm you. But don't be happy because evil spirits obey you. Be happy because you belong to God's kingdom."

Jesus Thanks His Father

Luke 10: 21-24

When Jesus' followers told him about their travels, he felt joy for them. He knew that God was with the people. So he got down on his knees and prayed, "My Father, thank you for what you have done. You have hidden your wisdom from the ones who think they know everything. Instead you've given your wisdom to the humble people. They are the ones who please you. My Father has given me everything. The only one who knows the Father is the Son. But the Son wants to tell others about the Father. When they know Him like I do, they will feel the same joy that is within me."

Then Jesus told his followers, "Many prophets and kings would love to see what you see. But you are the ones that God has chosen. You are really blessed!"

22

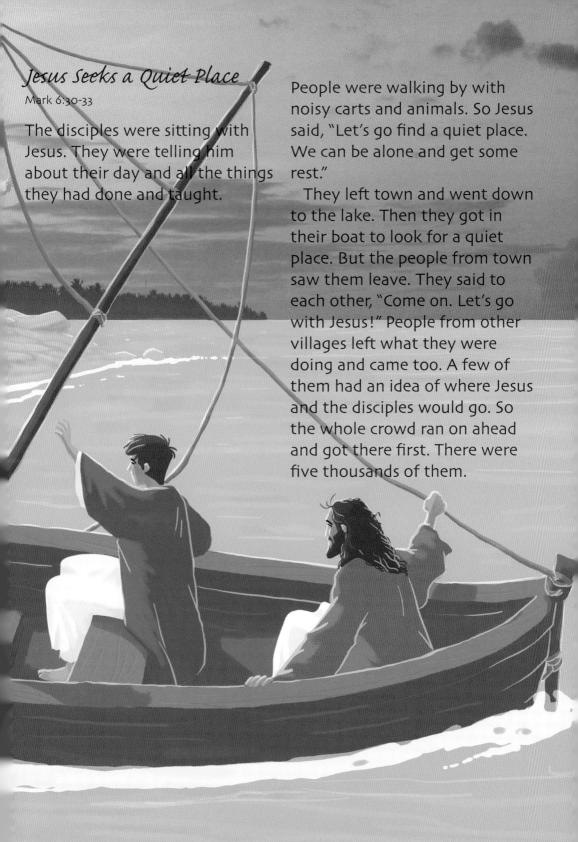

Jesus Seeks a Quiet Place

Mark 6:30-33

The disciples were sitting with Jesus. They were telling him about their day and all the things they had done and taught.

People were walking by with noisy carts and animals. So Jesus said, "Let's go find a quiet place. We can be alone and get some rest."

They left town and went down to the lake. Then they got in their boat to look for a quiet place. But the people from town saw them leave. They said to each other, "Come on. Let's go with Jesus!" People from other villages left what they were doing and came too. A few of them had an idea of where Jesus and the disciples would go. So the whole crowd ran on ahead and got there first. There were five thousands of them.

The Hungry People

Mark 6:34-38

When the disciples saw the big crowd, they groaned. But Jesus didn't mind. He felt compassion for them. They were like sheep without a shepherd. So he told them to come closer, and then he began to teach. Afternoon rolled around and the disciples were hungry. "Let's take a break," they told Jesus. "The people can go back to their villages and eat something."

But Jesus said, "Why don't you give them something to eat?"

"That's impossible," they replied. "It would cost a fortune to feed all these people!"

The disciple Andrew said, "Well, there is a boy here with some food. He has five loaves of bread and two fish. But that's not enough to feed five thousand people."

Five Loaves and Two Fish

Mark 6:39-44, John 6:8-14

Jesus told his disciples to have faith. "Tell the people to find a nice spot in the grass and sit down," he said. So the disciples obeyed. Once the people quieted down, Jesus stood up and took a loaf of bread in his hands. He bowed his head and gave thanks to God. Then he broke the bread and gave it to the people. He continued to pass the bread around until every single person

had a piece. Then he did the same with the fish.

There was plenty of food, and the people couldn't eat it all. Jesus told his disciples to not let anything go to waste. So they went around and gathered up the extra food in big baskets. The people were amazed when they saw Jesus' miracle. "How did he make so much food out of so little?" They asked each other. "He is a miracle-worker!"

29

Jesus Walks on Water

Mark 6:45-50

When the day was done, Jesus told his disciples to go home without him. He wanted to be by himself for a while. They said goodbye and got in their boat.

When all the crowds had left, Jesus climbed up to the side of the mountain and prayed.

That evening Jesus was still by himself on the mountainside. He could see the lake from where he sat, and he spotted

his disciples in their boat. The winds were very strong and they were having trouble rowing. So Jesus went down to help them. He started to walk on top of the water toward them. But when the disciples saw Jesus, they were scared. "It's a ghost," they cried out. They clung to each other's arm and trembled.

"It's me!" Jesus told them. "Don't be afraid."

Peter Lacks Faith

Matthew 14:28-33

Peter gathered his courage and spoke, "Lord, if it's really you, show me. Let me walk out to you on the water."

   Jesus answered, "Come on, Peter. Don't be afraid." Peter walked toward the edge of the boat. Then he stepped out onto the waves. He didn't sink, so he began to walk toward Jesus. But the wind picked up, and Peter got nervous. He started to look down at his feet. "I'm sinking, Jesus!" he cried. "Save me!"

   Jesus reached his hand out to Peter and lifted him up again.

   "Where did your faith go?" Jesus asked him. "If you had trusted me, you wouldn't have fallen. Why do you doubt?"

   Then Jesus and Peter walked back together toward the boat. The other disciples had been watching the whole thing. "You really are the Son of God!" they said. They bowed down at Jesus' feet and worshiped him.

A Woman's Faith

Matthew 15:21-28

Jesus was traveling with his disciples. A Canaanite woman walked behind them crying, "Lord, please have pity on me! I have a daughter, but she is full of evil spirits. Can you save her?" Jesus didn't say a word. The disciples told Jesus to send her away. But he said to her, "I have come to help the Israelites. They are like lost sheep. But you are a Canaanite."

"Please help me," she said again.

"Would it be right to take away food from children and give it to the dog instead?" Jesus asked her.

The woman replied, "You are right, Lord. But even dogs get the crumbs that fall from their owner's table."

Jesus rejoiced in his heart. He knew that she truly trusted him. "Dear woman," he said, "You do have faith after all! Go home— I've already given you what you asked for."

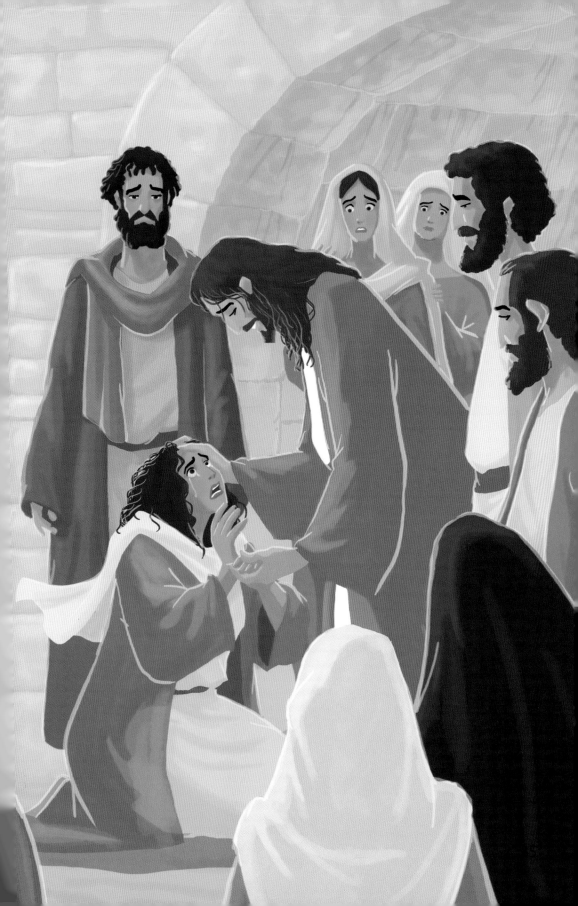

Jesus Heals a Blind Man

Mark 8:22-26

When Jesus and his disciples came to the town of Bethsaida, they saw some people coming towards them. It was a blind man being led by some of his friends. "Please heal this man," they asked Jesus. So Jesus took the man's hand and led him a little ways out of the village. Then he spit into the man's eyes. He put his hands over them, and then he took his hands away. "Can you see anything?" Jesus asked him.

"Yes Lord! I see some people, but they look like trees walking around."

So Jesus placed his hands on the man's eyes again.

"And can you see anything now?" Jesus asked him, as he took his hands away.

The man just stared. He saw everything as clear as day, and his eyes were full of wonder.

"You can go home now," Jesus told him. "But don't go through the village."

The Ten Lepers

Luke 17:11-19

Jesus was on his way to Jerusalem. He went through a village and saw ten men with leprosy. They cried out to him, "Jesus, have pity on us!"

Jesus went over to them and said, "Go to the priest and ask him for help." They obeyed Jesus and left. On their way to the priest, Jesus healed them.

They left to celebrate. But one man came back to Jesus. He was a Samaritan. He sang God's praises the whole way. When he saw Jesus, he bowed down at his feet. "Thank you, Lord. You have healed me," he said.

"Where are the others?" Jesus asked him. "You are a foreigner, and yet you are the only one who has come back to thank God. You can go now. Your faith has healed you."

Simon Shows True Faith

Matthew 16:13-19

Jesus and his disciples were near the town of Caesarea. While they were walking Jesus asked, "Who do people say that I am?"

His disciples answered, "Some people think you are John the Baptist raised from the dead. Other people think you are Elijah or Jeremiah or some other prophet."

Then Jesus asked, "Who do you think I am?"

Nobody said anything. But finally Simon Peter said, "You are the Son of God!"

Jesus smiled. "Simon, you are blessed. You could not have known this on your own. My Father in heaven told you. So I will change your name. It will be Peter, which means rock. And on that rock I will build my church. After you die, the church will go on. But I will give you the keys to my kingdom. God in heaven will be with you!"

41

Moses and Elijah Appear

Luke 9:28-36

Jesus went up on a mountain to pray. He brought Peter, John and James with him. While Jesus was praying, the other three fell asleep in the grass. Suddenly Moses and Elijah came down from heaven and spoke with Jesus. His plain clothes turned bright white. The three of them spoke about Jesus' death and what it would mean.

Peter, John and James heard their voices and woke up. They saw Jesus, Moses and Elijah in all their glory. They were amazed.

But Moses and Elijah knew it was time for them to go. "Don't go," Peter begged. "Let us make shelters for the three of you! We can all stay here together." But Peter didn't understand why they had really come.

God sent a dark cloud that passed over all of them. Then a voice spoke, saying, "This is my Son. Listen to what he tells you." Suddenly Moses and Elijah disappeared. Only Jesus was left. So the disciples stayed quiet. They didn't tell anyone about what happened.

Jesus Heals a Woman on the Sabbath

Luke 13:10-17

On Sunday Jesus was teaching in a meeting place. A woman was there whose back was bent. She could hardly see Jesus because she was forced to hunch over. "Come over here," Jesus told the woman. He put his hands on her, and the woman's back straightened. "You're well now!" Jesus said. The woman thanked God. But the man who was in charge of the meeting place was angry. He said to Jesus, "You can't heal someone on a Sunday. There are six other days you can heal her. Why do you have to do it today?"

So Jesus said, "If you had a thirsty donkey, you would give it a drink. If it were Sunday, would you let it go thirsty? This woman belongs to God. But she has been suffering eighteen years. I will heal her no matter what day of the week it is."

These words made the man feel ashamed. But everyone else in the crowd felt happy. They knew that Jesus was doing wonderful things.

The Death of Lazarus
John 11:1-16

Mary and Martha had a brother named Lazarus. He was one of Jesus' good friends. But one day Lazarus got very sick. He couldn't get out of bed. So Mary and Martha sent a message and told Jesus to come. Jesus got the news, but he didn't go right away. He knew that Lazarus would be alright.

Two days later Jesus told his disciples to come with him to see Lazarus. "But he lives in Judea," they answered. "Why do you want to go?"

Jesus answered, "Our friend Lazarus is asleep. I want to wake him up."

"Can't he wake up on his own?" his disciples asked. But they didn't understand what Jesus meant. "No, Lazarus is dead," he explained. But he will come back to us. I'm glad I didn't go sooner, because now you will have a good reason to put your faith in me. Let's go and I'll show you."

46

47

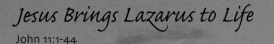

Jesus Brings Lazarus to Life

John 11:1-44

Martha saw that Jesus was coming. She ran out to meet him. Jesus said, "I am the one who can raise the dead! Anyone who puts their faith in me will live, even after death. Do you believe this, Martha?"

"Yes, Lord!" she replied. "I know that you are the Son of God."

Then Mary came out. She went to Jesus and kneeled down in front of him. "Lord, our brother is dead. If you had come sooner, I know he would've lived."

Jesus started to cry. Then he walked over to Lazarus' tomb. "Roll the stone away," he told them. But Martha said, "Lord, he's been dead for four days.

48

There will be a bad smell." The stone was rolled away. Jesus prayed, "Father, answer my prayer and let these people see that I am truly your Son."

Then Jesus said, "Lazarus, come out!"

A man came out of the tomb wrapped in burial cloth from head to foot. Jesus took the bandages off, and everyone saw it was Lazarus. Jesus had raised him from the dead!

The Cripple by the Water

John 5:1-9

Jesus was on his way to Jerusalem for a festival. As he came into the city, he walked by a large pool of water. The pool was surrounded by many sick, blind and crippled people. They were lying on decks around the pool. Some of them were swimming. Jesus saw a man lying near the edge of the water. He had been sick for thirty-eight years. Jesus felt compassion for him. "Do you want me to heal you?" he asked the man.

"Lord," the man replied, "I only want to go swimming

in the pool. I have no one to carry me in. And when I try to go by myself, I am so slow that someone always gets there before me." Jesus told him, "Pick up your mat and walk!" At that moment, the man was healed.

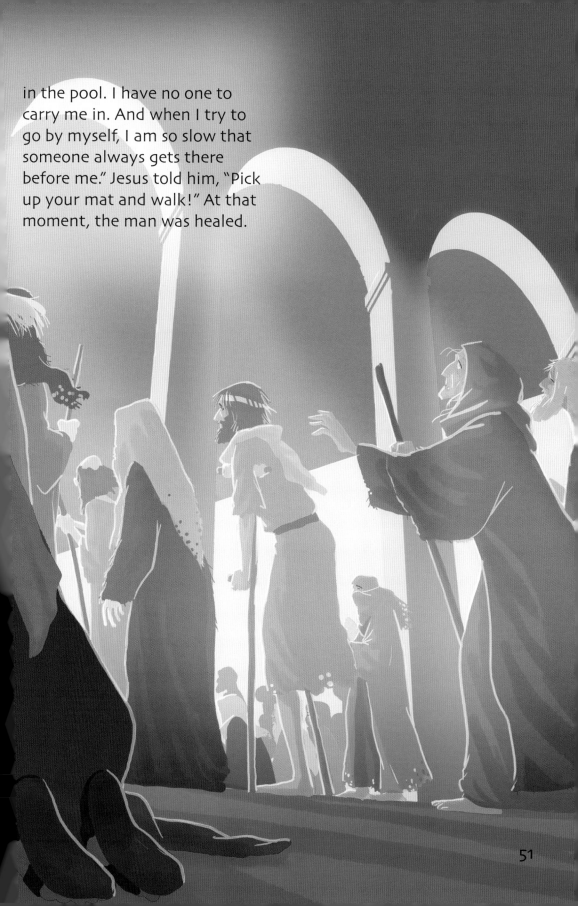

Little Man Zacchaeus

Luke 19:1-10

Zacchaeus was a man from Jericho. He collected people's taxes and made a lot of money. He heard that Jesus was coming to Jericho on his way to Jerusalem. So when Jesus finally came, Zacchaeus joined the big crowd that had gathered around him. But Zacchaeus was a little man. He couldn't see Jesus because there were too many people. So he found a tall sycamore tree and climbed up into its branches. Then he listened to Jesus while he spoke. Jesus spotted Zacchaeus in the tree. "Come here, Zacchaeus!" he said to him. "I want to stay with you today."

Everyone in the crowd started to complain. Nobody liked Zacchaeus because he was a tax collector. "Why does Jesus want to stay with a sinner like him?" But Zacchaeus was very excited. He came down the tree and invited Jesus to his home. After spending the day together, Zacchaeus was like a new man. He said to Jesus, "I'm giving up all my riches. I will give what I have to the poor. And I will pay back four times as much to everyone I cheated."

Jesus said, "Because of this, you and your family are saved. You have heard my message in your heart. Taking from people made you rich. But giving to people is what brings true joy."

53

The Big Parade

Luke 19:28-38

Jesus was nearing Jerusalem. He sent two of his disciples ahead of him. "Go into the next village," he instructed them. "There you'll see a donkey tied to a pole. Untie the donkey and bring it back to me. If anyone asks why you are taking it, tell them the Lord needs it."

The disciples went and found the donkey Jesus was talking about. As they began to untie it, the owner of the donkey snapped at them. "What do you think you're doing?" he asked. But the man let them go when they told him the Lord needed it.

They brought the donkey to Jesus, and he climbed on its back. Then he rode down the Mount of Olives toward Jerusalem.

The people were waiting for him down below. They had taken large palm tree leaves and waved them like flags. They also put their clothes down on the ground to make a path for Jesus. The disciples cheered and sang praises alongside the people. "Blessed is the king our Lord! Peace in heaven and glory to God!"

Jerusalem! Jerusalem!

Luke 19:39-44

As Jesus rode into Jerusalem, the people cheered so loudly that the noise shook the buildings. They praised God with all their might. But the Pharisees were irritated. "Make those people stop shouting," they demanded. Jesus said to them, "Even if they kept quiet, the stones themselves would begin to sing!" And so the people went right on singing God's praises. Then Jesus cried out, "Jerusalem! God has come to save you, but still the truth is hidden from your eyes. You don't know the true meaning of peace. If you know me, then you will know peace. Enemies cannot attack you, and armies cannot tear you down. Remember that God has come to save you!"

Healing in the Temple
Matthew 21:14-16

The first thing Jesus did in
Jerusalem was visit the temple.
Many people followed him.
He healed every blind, sick
or crippled person that came
to him. But the teachers and

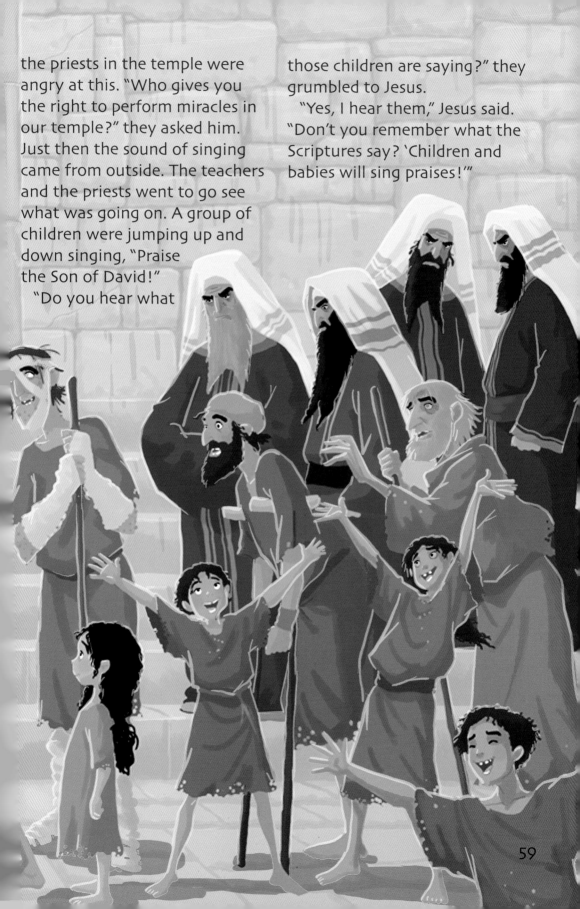

the priests in the temple were angry at this. "Who gives you the right to perform miracles in our temple?" they asked him. Just then the sound of singing came from outside. The teachers and the priests went to go see what was going on. A group of children were jumping up and down singing, "Praise the Son of David!"

"Do you hear what those children are saying?" they grumbled to Jesus.

"Yes, I hear them," Jesus said. "Don't you remember what the Scriptures say? 'Children and babies will sing praises!'"

Judas Betrays Jesus
Matthew 26:1-5, 14-16

That night Jesus was with his disciples. He told them, "Two days from now is the festival for Passover. That's the day your Lord will be taken from you. On that day my enemies will nail me to a cross."

Meanwhile, the leaders of Jerusalem had come together to plot against Jesus. They met in secret and planned Jesus' death. "We can't do it during the festival," they said to one another. "There are too many people, and they might riot!" So they schemed about where and when they would arrest Jesus. Just then Judas Iscariot, one of Jesus' twelve disciples, walked in the door. "If you pay me," he told them. "I will help you get Jesus." The leaders agreed and paid Judas thirty silver coins.

The Contemporary Bible Series